The *Family Christmas*
Song Book

The *Family Christmas* Song Book

A Family Media Co. Anthology

Yonkers, New York

Library of Congress Cataloging-in-Publication Data

ISBN 0-9709378-0-6

Printed in Korea

Contents

Contents (continued)

Contents (continued)

This musical anthology would not have been
possible without the help and support of
Mary Pastirchak,
David Pastirchak,
Grace Maher,
and Rosemarie Gawelko

FOREWARD

Like most parents in busy America I never had the time to sit down and learn <u>all</u> of the words to those wonderful carols we hear at Christmas time. But how could I guide and encourage my children in singing if I didn't know the words myself? I designed *The Family Christmas Song Book* to be a colorful Christmas song reference that will remain on your living room table throughout the Christmas season.

The Family Christmas Song Book has something for every family member. Children of all ages can browse through photographs depicting the baby Jesus, the Nativity, Santa Claus, and other families celebrating the Christmas season. Mothers, fathers, grandparents, aunts, and uncles can use *The Family Christmas Song Book* to teach children the words to their favorite Christmas songs. Shoppers now have a gift that's suitable for any family member or the whole family.

At the end of the Christmas season *The Family Christmas Song Book* can be packed and stored with other Christmas items and used for singing Christmas carols together in future Christmas seasons.

The book requires one note on musical notation. Additional verses appear at the end of most Christmas carols. If the word *Chorus* or *Refrain* appear at the end of a verse you will need to find the word *Chorus or Refrain* in the body of the music and sing these measures before you move on to the next verse.

Angels We Have Heard on High

French Carol

An - gels we have heard on high, Sweet - ly sing - ing on the plain. And the moun - tains in re - ply Ech - o - ing their joy - ous strain: Glo - - - -

Angels We Have Heard on High

ri - a

in ex - cel - sius de - o.   de - - o.

Shepherds why this jubilee?
Why your joyful strains prolong?
What the gladsome tidings be
Which inspire your heav'nly song?
Chorus

Come to Bethlehem and see
Him whose birth the angels sing;
Come adore on bended knee
Christ, the Lord, the newborn King.
Chorus

See Him in a manger laid,
Whom the choir of angels praise;
Holy Spirit lend thine aid,
While our hearts in love we raise.
Chorus

Away In A Manger

German Carol

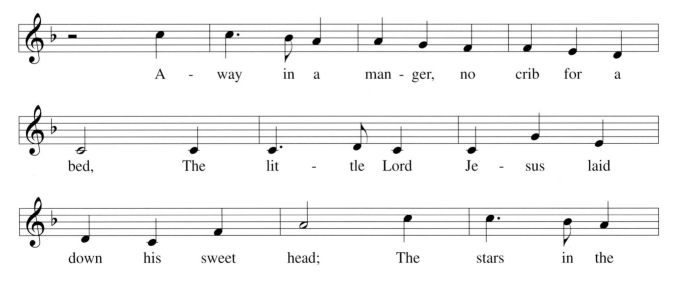

A - way   in a   man - ger,   no   crib   for   a

bed,   The   lit - tle   Lord   Je - sus   laid

down   his   sweet   head;   The   stars   in   the

Away In A Manger

sky looked down where he lay, The
lit - tle Lord Je - sus a - sleep in the hay.

The cattle are lowing, the baby awakes,
But little Lord Jesus, no crying he makes.
I love Thee, Lord Jesus, look down from the sky,
And stay by my cradle 'til morning is nigh.

Be near me, Lord Jesus, I ask Thee to stay
Close by me forever, and love me, I pray.
Bless all the dear children in thy tender care,
And fit us for heaven to live with Thee there.

Bring A Torch, Jeanette, Isabella

French Carol

Bring a Torch, Jeannette, Isabella

call - ing: Ah!   Ah!   beau - ti - ful

is   the   moth - er,   Ah!   Ah!

beau - ti - ful   is   her   son!

It is wrong when the child is sleeping,
It is wrong to talk so loud;
Silence, all, as you gather around,
Lest your noise should waken Jesus:
Hush! Hush! see how fast he slumbers:
Hush! Hush! see how fast he sleeps!

Softly to the little stable,
Softly for a moment come;
Look and see how charming is Jesus,
How he is white, his cheeks are rosy!
Hush! Hush! see how the child
                                    is sleeping;
Hush! Hush! see how he smiles
                                    in his dreams.

Deck the Hall

Welsh Carol

Deck the hall with boughs of hol - ly, Fa - la - la - la la, la

la - la - la. 'Tis the sea - son to be jol - ly,

Fa - la - la - la la, la la - la - la. Don we now our

gay ap - par - rel, Fa - la - la, la - la - la, la - la - la.

Troll the an - cient Yule - tide car - ol, Fa - la - la - la la, la - la - la - la.

See the blazing Yule before us,
Fa-la-la-la-la, la-la-la-la.
Strike the harp and join the chorus.
Fa-la-la-la-la, la-la-la-la.
Follow me in merry measure,
Fa-la-la, la-la-la, la-la-la.
While I tell of Yuletide treasure,
Fa-la-la-la-la, la-la-la-la.

Fast away the old year passes,
Fa-la-la-la-la, la-la-la-la.
Hail the new, ye lads and lasses,
Fa-la-la-la-la, la-la-la-la.
Sing we joyous all together,
Fa-la-la, la-la-la, la-la-la.
Heedless of the wind and weather,
Fa-la-la-la-la, la-la-la-la.

Dona Nobis Pacem

(Grant Us Peace)

Traditional German Carol

Dona Nobis Pacem

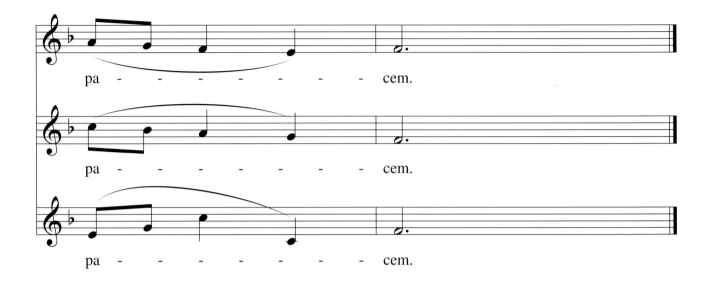

pa - - - - - - cem.

pa - - - - - - cem.

pa - - - - - - cem.

The First Noel

English Carol

The first No - el the an - gel did

say, Was to cer - tain poor shep - herds in

fields as they lay; In fields where

they lay keep - ing their sheep, On a

cold win - ter's night that was so

chorus

deep. No - - el, No - el, No -

The First Noel

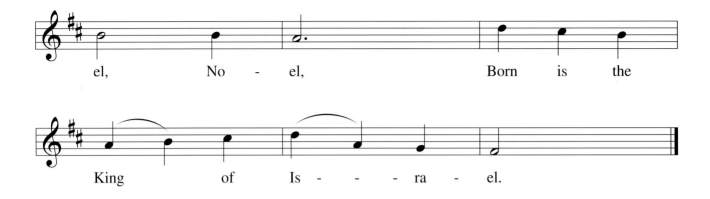

el,　　No　-　el,　　　　　　Born　is　the

King　　of　Is　-　-　-　ra　-　el.

They looked up and saw a star,
Shining in the east beyond them far,
And to the earth it gave great light,
And so it continued both day and night.
Chorus

This star drew nigh to the northwest,
O'er Bethlehem it took its rest,
And there it did both stop and stay,
Right over the place where Jesus lay.
Chorus

Frosty The Snow Man

Words and Music by
STEVE NELSON
and JACK ROLLINS

FROS - TY, THE SNOW MAN was a

mp

jol - ly hap - py soul. With a corn cob pipe and a

Frosty The Snowman

but - ton nose and two eyes made out of coal.

mf

FROS - TY THE SNOW MAN is a fair - y tale, they

say. He was made of snow but the chil - dren know how he

came to life one day. There must have been some

mp

mag - ic in that old silk hat they found. For

cresc.

when they placed it on his head he be - gan to dance a -

rit. **mf** *a tempo*

round. Oh, FROS - TY THE SNOW MAN was a -

live as he could be. And the chil - dren say he could

Frosty The Snowman

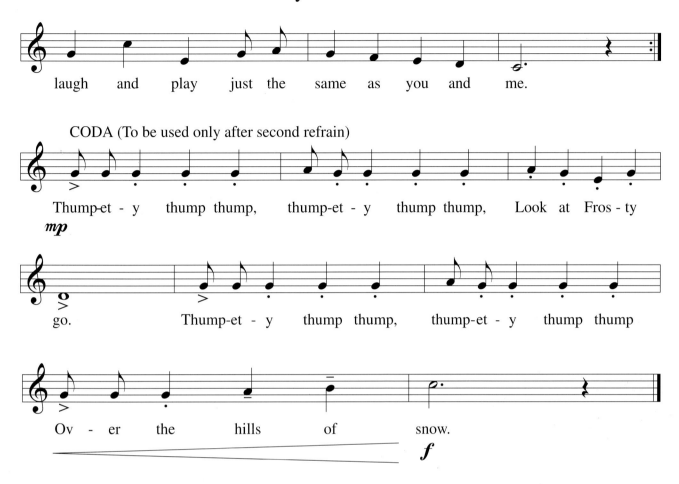

laugh and play just the same as you and me.

CODA (To be used only after second refrain)

Thump-et - y thump thump, thump-et - y thump thump, Look at Fros - ty

mp

go. Thump-et - y thump thump, thump-et - y thump thump

Ov - er the hills of snow.

f

FROS-TY THE SNOW MAN knew the sun was hot that day,
So he said "Let's run and we'll have some fun now be-fore I
melt a-way." Down to the vil-lage, with a broom-stick in his
hand, Run-ning here and there all a-round the square, say-in',
"catch me if you can." He led them down the streets of town
right to the traf-fic cop. And he on-ly paused a mo-ment when
he heard him hol-ler "stop"! For FROS-TY THE SNOW MAN
had to hur-ry on his way But he waved good-bye say-in', "Don't
you cry, I'll be back a-gain some day."

Go Tell It On The Mountain

African-American Carol

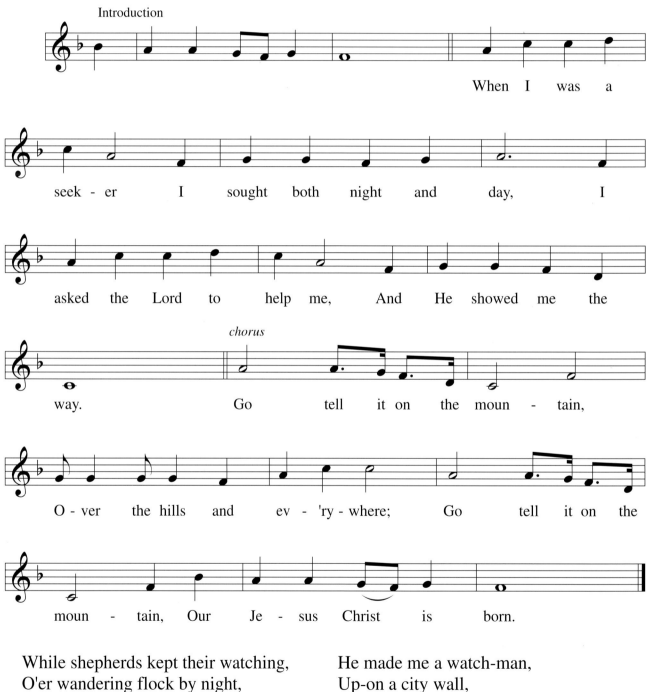

When I was a seek - er I sought both night and day, I asked the Lord to help me, And He showed me the way.

chorus
Go tell it on the moun - tain, O - ver the hills and ev - 'ry - where; Go tell it on the moun - tain, Our Je - sus Christ is born.

While shepherds kept their watching,
O'er wandering flock by night,
Behold! from out of heaven,
There shown a holy light.
  Chorus

He made me a watch-man,
Up-on a city wall,
And if I am a Chris-tian,
I am the least of all.
  Chorus

God Rest Ye Merry, Gentlemen

Traditional English

Introduction

God rest you mer - ry, gen - tle - men, Let

noth - ing you dis - may, Re - mem - ber Christ our

Sa - vior was born on Christ - mas Day; To

save us all from Sa - tan's power when we were gone a -

Chorus

stray O tid - ings of com - fort and joy, com - fort and

God Rest Ye Merry, Gentlemen

joy; O tid - ings of com - fort and joy.

In Bethlehem in Jewry this blessed babe was born,
And laid within a manger upon this blessed morn.
To which his mother Mary nothing did take in scorn.
Chorus

From God our heavenly Father a blessed Angel came.
And unto certain shepherds brought tidings of the same.
How that in Bethlehem was born the Son of God by name.
Chorus

"Fear not," then said the angel, "let nothing you affright,
This day is born a Savior, of virtue, power and might.
So frequently to vanquish all the friends of Satan quite".
Chorus

The shepherds at those tidings rejoiced much in mind.
And left their flocks a-feeding in tempest, storm, and wind,
And went to Bethlehem straightway, This blessed Babe to find.
Chorus

But when to Bethlehem they came whereat this infant lay,
They found him in a manger, where oxen feed on hay,
His mother Mary kneeling unto the Lord did pray.
Chorus

Now to the Lord sing praises all you within this place,
And with true love and brotherhood each other now embrace,
This holy tide of Christmas all others doth deface.
Chorus

Good King Wenceslas

JOHN M. NEALE

Good King Wen - cel - las looked out On the Feast of

Ste - phen, When the snow lay round a - bout,

Deep and crisp and e - ven. Bright - ly shone the

Good King Wenceslas

moon that night, Through the frost was cru - el, When a poor man

came in sight, Gath - 'ring win - ter fu - - - el.

"Hither, page, and stand by me,
If thou know'st it, telling,
Yonder peasant, who is he?
Where and what his dwelling?"
"Sire, he lives a good league hence,
Underneath the mountain;
Right against the forest fence,
By St. Agnes fountain!"

"Bring me flesh and bring me wine,
Bring me pine logs hither;
Thou and I will see him dine
When we bear them hither."
Page and monarch forth they went,
Forth they went together
Through the rude wind's wild lament
And the bitter weather.

"Sire, the night is darker now,
And the wind blows stronger.
Fails my heart, I know not how,
I can go no longer."
"Mark my footsteps good, my page,
Tread thou in them boldly.
Thou shalt find the winter's rage
Freeze thy blood less coldly."

In his master's steps he trod,
Where the snow lay dinted.
Heat was in the very sod
which the saint had printed.
Therefore, Christian men be sure,
Wealth or rank possessing,
Ye who now will bless the poor,
Shall youselves find blessing.

Hark! The Herald Angels Sing

CHARLES WESLEY

FELIX MENDELSSOHN

Hark! The her - ald an - gels sing, "Glo - ry to the new - born King; Peace on earth, and mer - cy mild, God and sin - ners rec - on - ciled!" Joy - ful, all ye na - tions, rise, Join the tri - umph of the skies; With th'an - gel - ic hosts pro - claim, "Christ is born in Beth - le - hem!"

Chorus

Hark! The her - ald an - gels sing, "Glo - ry to the new - born King."

Christ, by highest heaven adored;	Hail, the heavenborn Prince of Peace!
Christ the everlasting Lord;	Hail, the Sun of Righteousness!
Come, Desire of Nations, come,	Light and life to all He brings,
Fix in us thy humble home.	Risen with healing in His wings;
Veiled in flesh the Godhead see;	Mild He lays His glory by,
Hail th'Incarnate Deity,	Born that man no more may die,
Pleased as man with man to dwell;	Born to raise the sons of earth,
Jesus, our Emmanuel.	Born to give them second birth.

Have Yourself
A Merry Little Christmas

Sacred Lyrics by
HUGH MARTIN and JOHN FRICKE

Words and Music by
HUGH MARTIN and RALPH BLANE

Have Yourself A Merry Little Christmas

make the yule - tide gay. From now on, our

trou - bles will be miles a - way.

Here we are as in old - en days, hap - py gold - en days of

yore. Faith - ful friends, who are dear to us, gath - er

near to us once more. Through the years, we

all will be to - geth - er, if the Fates al - low.

Hang a shin - ing star up - on the high - est bough,

Have Yourself A Merry Little Christmas

and have your - self a mer - ry lit - tle Christ - mas

1.

now.

2.

now.

[Sacred Lyrics]

𝄋 *Have your-self a bless-ed lit-tle Christ-mas,*
Christ the King is born. Let your voic-es
ring up-on this hap-py morn. Have your-self
a bless-ed lit-tle Christ-mas, ser-e-nade the
earth. Tell the world we cel-e-brate the Sav-
ior's birth. Let us gath-er to sing to Him, and
to bring to Him our praise: Son of God and
a friend of all to the end of all our days. Let
us all pro-claim the joy-ous tid-ings, voic-es
raised on high. Send this car-ol soar-ing up
in-to the sky, this ver-y mer-ry, bless-ed Christ-
mas lul-la-by.

✳ *2. Sing ho-san-nas, hymns and hal-le-lu-jahs,*
as to Him we bow. Make this mu-sic might-y
as the heavn's al-low, and have your-self a
bless-ed lit-tle Christ-mas now.

Here Comes Santa Claus

(Right Down Santa Claus Lane)

Words and Music by
GENE AUTRY and
OAKLEY HALDEMAN

f Here Comes San-ta Claus! Here Comes San-ta Claus!

Right down San-ta Claus Lane! Vix-en and Blit-zen and

Here Comes Santa Claus (Right Down Santa Claus Lane)

all his rein - deer are pull - ing on the rein.

Bells are ring - ing, chil - dren sing - ing all is mer - ry and

bright. Hang your stock - ings and say your pray'rs, 'Cause

San - ta Claus comes to - night.

Here Comes San-ta Claus! Here Comes San-ta Claus! Right down San-ta Claus Lane! He's got a bag that is filled with toys for the boys and girls a-gain. Hear those sleigh-bells jin-gle jan-gle, what a beau-ti-ful sight. Jump in bed, cov-er up your head, 'Cause San-ta Claus comes to-night.

Here Comes San-ta Claus! Here Comes San-ta Claus! Right down San-ta Claus Lane! He does-n't care if you're rich or poor for he loves you just the same. San-ta knows that we're God's chil-dren that makes ev-'ry-thing right. Fill your hearts with a Christ-mas cheer, 'Cause San-ta Claus comes to-night.

Here Comes San-ta Claus! Here Comes San-ta Claus! Right down San-ta Claus Lane! He'll come a-round when the chimes ring out then it's Christ-mas morn a-gain. Peace on earth will come to all if we just fol-low the light. Let's give thanks to the Lord a-bove, 'Cause San-ta Claus comes to-night.

34

Here We Come A-Caroling

Traditional English Carol

Here we come a-car-ol-ing A-mong the leaves so green; Here we come a-wan-d'ring So fair to be seen.

Chorus

Love and joy come to you, And to you glad Christ-mas too, And God bless you and send you a Hap-py New Year, And God send you a Hap-py New Year.

We are not daily beggars
That beg from door to door
But we are neighbor's children,
Whom you have seen before.
 Chorus

God bless the Master of this house,
Likewise the Mistress too;
And all the little children
That round the table go.
 Chorus

35

A Holly Jolly Christmas

Words and Music by
Johnny Marks

Introduction

Have A HOL - LY JOL - LY CHRIST - MAS, it's the

best time of the year. I don't know if

there'll be snow but have a cup of cheer. Have A

HOL - LY JOL - LY CHRIST - MAS, and when you walk down the street

Say hel - lo to friends you know and

ev - 'ry - one you meet. Oh, ho, the

A Holly Jolly Christmas

mis - tle - toe hung where you can see.

Some - bod - y waits for you, kiss her once for

me. Have A HOL - LY JOL - LY CHRIST-MAS, and in

case you did - n't hear Oh, by gol - ly, have A

1
HOL - LY JOL - LY CHRIST-MAS this year. Have a

2
CHRIST - MAS this year.

37

I Saw Three Ships

Traditional English Carol

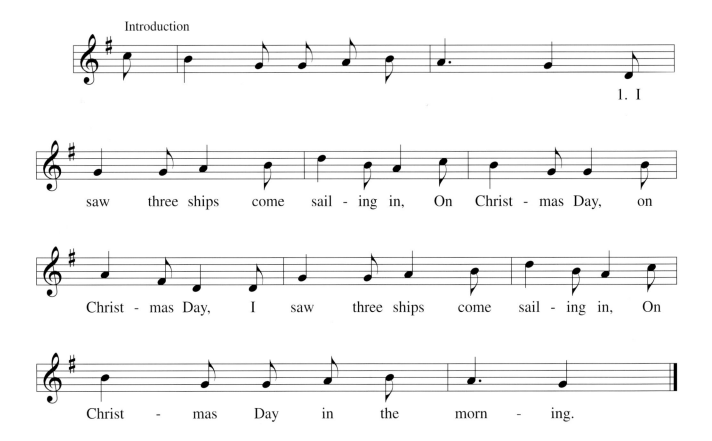

2. And what was in those ships all three?
3. The Virgin Mary and Christ were there,
4. Pray, whither sailed those ships all three?
5. O they sailed into Bethlehem,
6. And all the bells on earth shall ring,
7. And all the angels in Heaven shall sing,
8. And all the souls on earth shall sing,
9. Then let us all rejoice amain,

It Came Upon A Midnight Clear

Edmund Sears

Richard S. Willis

It Came Upon a Midnight Clear

Still through the cloven skies they come with peaceful wings unfurled,
And still their heavenly music floats over all the weary world.
Above its sad and lowly plain they bend on hovering wing,
and ever over its Babel sounds the blessed angels sing.

Yet with the woes of sin and strife the world has suffered long.
Beneath the angel-strain have rolled two thousand years of wrong.
And man, at war with man, hears not the love-song which they bring.
Oh hush the noise, ye men of strife, and hear the angels sing.

And ye, beneath life's crushing load, whose forms are bending low,
Who toil along the climbing way with weary steps and slow,
Look up! for glad and golden hours come swiftly on the wing.
O rest beside the weary road and hear the angels sing.

For lo! the days are hastening on, by prophet bards foretold,
When with the ever-circling years comes round the Age of Gold.
When peace shall over all the earth its ancient splendors fling,
And the whole world give back the song which now the angels sing.

IT'S THE MOST WONDERFUL TIME OF THE YEAR

By EDDIE POLA and GEORGE WYLE

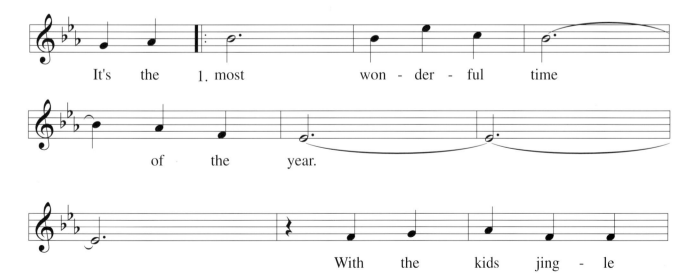

It's the 1. most won-der-ful time of the year.

With the kids jing-le

It's The Most Wonderful Time Of The Year

bell - ing, and ev - 'ry - one tell - ing you,

"Be of good cheer."

It's the most won - der - ful

time of the year.

It's the

There'll be par - ties for host - ing, marsh -

mal - lows for toast - ing and car - ol - ing

out in the snow. There'll be

It's The Most Wonderful Time Of The Year

scar - y ghost sto - ries and tales of the

glo - ries of Christ - mas - es long long a -

go.

It's the most won - der - ful

time of the year.

There'll be

much mis - tle - toe - ing and hearts will be

glow - ing, when loved ones are near.

It's the most

It's The Most Wonderful Time Of The Year

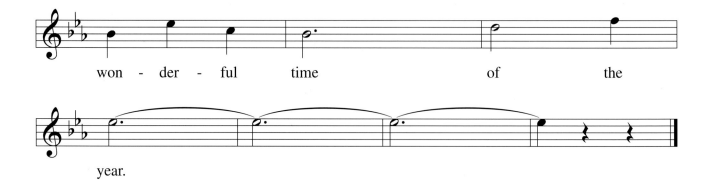

won - der - ful   time   of   the

year.

2. hap-hap-pi-est sea-son of all.
   With those hol-i-day greet-ings,
   and gay hap-py meet-ings
   when friends come to call,
   it's the hap-hap-pi-est sea-son of all.

Jingle Bells

Words and music by
James Pierpont

1. Dash - ing through the snow, In a one - horse o - pen

sleigh, And o'er the fields we go,

Laugh - ing all the way. The bells on Bob - tail

Jingle Bells

ring, They're mak - ing spir - its bright, What

fun it is to ride and sing a sleigh - ing song to -

Chorus

night! Jin - gle bells! Jin - gle bells!

Jin - gle all the way! Oh, what fun it

is to ride in a one - horse o - pen sleigh, ——

Jin - gle bells! Jin - gle bells! Jin - gle all the way!

Oh, what fun it is to ride in a one - horse o - pen sleigh!

A day or so ago,
I thought I'd take a ride,
And soon Miss Fannie Bright
Was seated by my side.
The horse was lean and lank,
Misfortune seemed his lot,
He got into a drifted bank,
And we? We got upsot!
Chorus

Now the ground is white,
Go it while you're young,
Take the girls tonight,
And sing this sleighing song.
Just get a bob-tailed nag,
Two-forty for his speed,
Then hitch him to an open sleigh,
And crack! You'll take the lead.
Chorus

46

Jingle-Bell Rock

Words and Music by
JOE BEAL
and JIM BOOTHE

Jingle-Bell Rock

right — time — To rock the night a - way — Jin - gle - bell — time — is a

swell time —— To go gli - din' in a one - horse sleigh ——

Gid - dy - ap, jin - gle horse pick up your feet —— Jin - gle a - round the

clock Mix and min - gle in a jin - gl - in' beat ——

That's the JIN - GLE - BELL ROCK.—— That's the Jin - gle - bell,

That's the JIN - GLE - BELL ROCK. ——

48

Jolly Old Saint Nicholas

Traditional American Carol

1. Jol - ly old Saint Nich - o - las,
Lean your ear this way! Don't you tell a
sin - gle soul What I'm going to say;
Christ - mas Eve is com - ing soon; Now, you dear old man,
Whis - per what you'll bring to me; Tell me if you can.

When the clock is striking twelve,
When I'm fast asleep,
Down the chimney broad and black,
With your pack you'll creep.
All the stockings you will find
Hanging in a row.
Mine will be the shortest one,
You'll be sure to know.

Johnny wants a pair of skates;
Suzy wants a dolly;
Nelly wants a story book,
She thinks dolls are folly.
As for me, my little brain
Isn't very bright,
Choose for me old Santa Claus,
What you think is right.

Joy to the World

Issac Watts   George F. Handel

Joy to the world! The Lord is come; Let earth receive her King. Let ev'ry heart pre-

Joy to the World

pare — him — room, — And heav'n and na - ture —
sing, And — heav'n and na - ture — sing, And —
heav'n — and heav'n — and na - ture sing.

Joy to the world! The Savior reigns;
Let men their songs employ;
While fields and floods, rocks and hills and plains
Repeat the sounding joy,
Repeat the sounding Joy,
Repeat, repeat the sounding joy.

He rules the world with truth and grace,
And makes the nations prove
The glories of His righteousness,
And wonders of His love,
And wonders of His love,
And wonders, and wonders of His Love.

Let It Snow! Let It Snow! Let It Snow!

Lyric by
SAMMY CAHN

Music by
JULE STYNE

(Rhythmic, but not too fast)

Oh! the weath-er out-side is fright-ful But the fire is so de-light-ful And since we've no place to go, LET IT SNOW! LET IT SNOW! LET IT SNOW! It does-n't show signs of stop-ping And I brought some corn for pop-ping; The lights are turned 'way down low, LET IT

Let It Snow! Let It Snow! Let It Snow!

SNOW! LET IT SNOW! LET IT SNOW! When we fin-al-ly kiss good-

night, How I'll hate go-ing out in the storm! But if

you'll real-ly hold me tight All the way home I'll be

warm. The fi-re is slow-ly dy-ing And, my

dear, we're still good-bye-ing, But as long as you love me

so LET IT SNOW! LET IT SNOW! LET IT SNOW! Oh the SNOW!

The Little Drummer Boy

Words and Music by
KATHERINE DAVIS,
HENRY ONORATI
and HARRY SIMEONE

The Little Drummer Boy

rum pum pum pum, _____ So to

hon - or Him pa - rum pum pum pum, _____

1. when we come. _____

2. on my drum. _____

Mar - - - y

nod - ded pa - rum pum pum pum, _____

The Ox and Lamb Kept time pa - rum pum pum pum, _____

_____ I played my drum for Him pa -

The Little Drummer Boy

rum pum pum pum,   I played my

best for Him pa - rum pum pum pum rum pum pum pum

rum pum pum pum.

Then He smiled at me pa -

rum pum pum pum   me and my drum.

Lit-tle Ba-by pa-rum pum pum pum,
I am a poor boy too, pa-rum pum pum pum,
I have no gift to bring pa-rum pum pum pum,
That's fit to give our King pa-rum pum pum pum
rum pum pum pum rum pum pum pum, Shall I
play for you? pa-rum pum pum pum,

O Christmas Tree

Traditional German Carol

Introduction

Christ - mas tree, O Christ - mas tree, How true you stand un -

chang - ing. O Christ - mas tree, O Christ - mas tree, How

O Christmas Tree

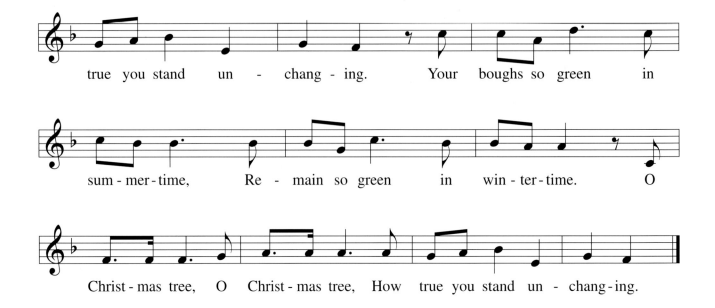

true you stand un - chang - ing. Your boughs so green in sum - mer - time, Re - main so green in win - ter - time. O Christ - mas tree, O Christ - mas tree, How true you stand un - chang - ing.

O Christmas tree, O Christmas tree,
Thy message is enduring;
O Christmas tree, O Christmas tree,
Thy message is enduring.
So long ago in Bethlehem
Was born the Savior of all men;
O Christmas tree, O Christmas tree,
Thy message is enduring.

O Christmas tree, O Christmas tree,
Thy faith is so unchanging;
O Christmas tree, O Christmas tree,
Thy faith is so unchanging.
A symbol sent from God above,
Proclaiming Him the Lord of Love;
O Christmas tree, O Christmas tree,
How true you stand unchanging.

O Come All Ye Faithful

John Reading

1. O come, all ye faith - ful,
1. *Ad - es - te fi - del - es,*

joy - ful and tri - um - phant, O come ye, O
lae - ti tri - um - phan - tes, Ve - ni - te, Ve -

come ye to Beth - le - hem:
ni - te in Beth - le - hem:

Come and be - hold Him, born the King of
Na - tum vi - de te, Re - gem an - ge -

an - gels: O come, let us a - dore Him, O
lo - rum: Ve - ni - te ad - o - re - mus, Ve -

come, let us a - dore Him, O come, let us a -
ni - te ad - o - re - mus, Ve - ni - te ad - o -

dore Him, Christ the Lord
re - mus, Do - mi - num.

59

O Holy Night

Adolphe C. Adam

O Holy Night

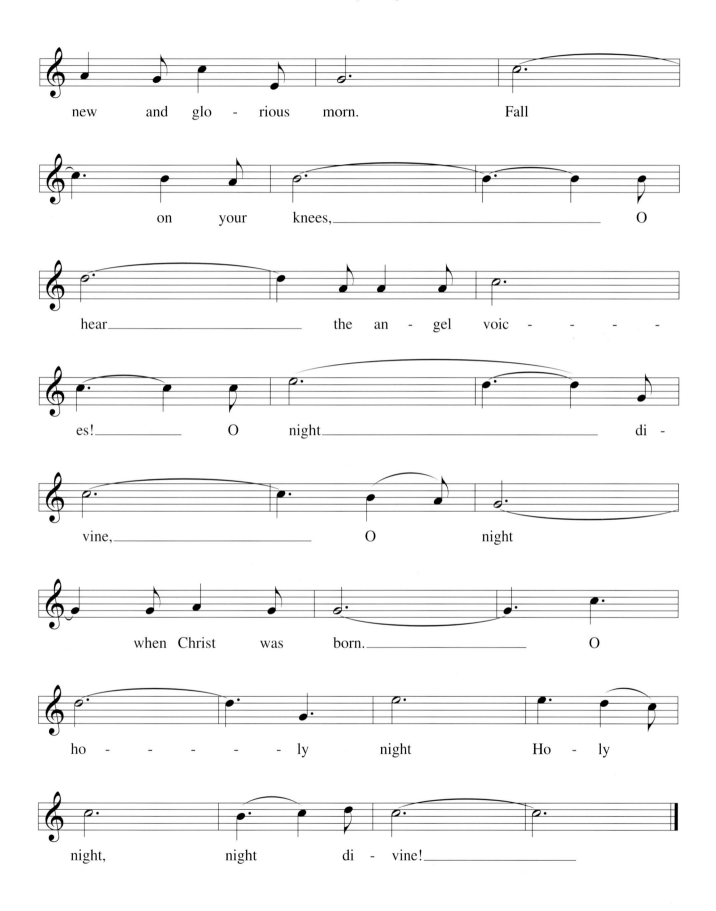

O Little Town of Bethlehem

Phillips Brooks

Lewis Redner

O Little Town of Bethlehem

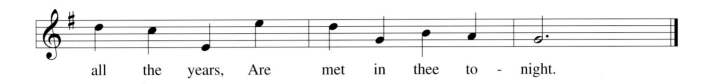

all the years, Are met in thee to - night.

For Christ is born of Ma-ry
And gath-ered all a-bove,
While mor-tals sleep, the angels keep
Their watch of won-d'ring love.
O morn-ing stars, to-geth-er
Pro-claim the ho-ly birth,
And prais-es sing to God the King,
And peace to men on earth.

Rock-in' Around the Christmas Tree

Words and Music by
Johnny Marks

Introduction

ROCK-IN' A - ROUND THE CHRIST-MAS TREE at the

Rockin' Around the Christmas Tree

Christ - mas par - ty hop. Mis - tle - toe hung where

you can see ev - 'ry cou - ple tries to stop.

ROCK - IN' A - ROUND THE CHRIST - MAS TREE, let the Christ-mas spir - it ring.

Lat - er we'll have some pun - kin pie and we'll

do some car - ol - ing. You will get a

sen - ti - men - tal feel - ing when you hear

voic - es sing - ing "Let's be jol - ly, Deck the halls with

boughs of hol - ly". ROCK - 'IN' A - ROUND THE CHRIST - MAS TREE, have a

Rockin' Around the Christmas Tree

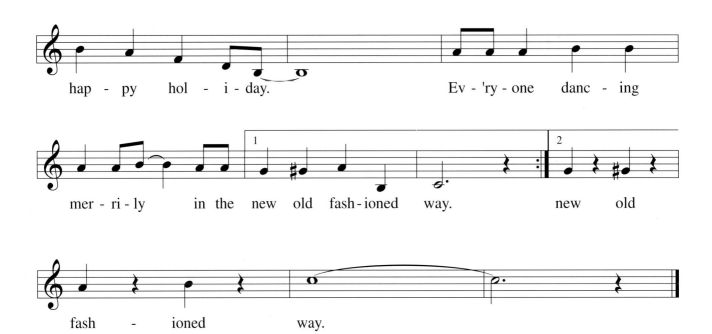

hap - py hol - i - day.   Ev - 'ry - one   danc - ing

mer - ri - ly   in the new old fash - ioned way.   new old

fash - ioned   way.

Rudolph The Red-Nosed Reindeer

Words and Music by
Johnny Marks

Introduction

You know Dash - er and Danc - er and Pranc - er and Vix - en,

Com - et and Cu - pid and Don - ner and Blitz - en, but do you re -

call the most fa - mous rein - deer of all.

Ru - dolph, the red - nosed rein - deer had a ver - y shin - y

nose, and if you ev - er saw it,

you would e - ven say it glows. All of the oth - er

Rudolph The Red-Nosed Reindeer

rein - deer used to laugh and call him names,

they nev - er let poor Ru - dolph join in an - y rein - deer

games. Then one fog - gy Christ - mas Eve,

San - ta came to say, "Ru - dolph, with your

nose so bright, won't you guide my sleigh to - night?"

Then how the rein - deer loved him as they shout - ed out with glee:

1
"Ru - dolph, the red - nosed rein - deer, you'll go down in his - to - ry!"

2
you'll go down in his - to - ry!"

Santa Claus is Comin' To Town

Words and Music by
HAVEN GILLESPIE and
J. FRED COOTS

1. I just came back from a love-ly trip A - long the Milk-y

mf

Way, I stopped off at the North Pole To

Santa Claus Is Comin' To Town

spend a hol - i - day; I called on dear old

San - ta Claus To see what I could see, He

took me to his work - shop And told his plans to

CHORUS *(delicato)*

me. So, You bet - ter watch out, you bet-ter not cry,

Bet - ter not pout, I'm tell-ing you why: San - ta Claus is

com - in' to town. He's

mak - ing a list and check-ing it twice, Gon-na find out who's

naught - y and nice, San - ta Claus is com - in' to

70

Santa Claus Is Comin' To Town

town. He sees you when you're sleep-in', He knows when you're a-wake, He knows if you've been bad or good, So be good for good-ness sake. Oh! You bet-ter watch out, you bet-ter not cry, Bet-ter not pout, I'm tell-ing you why: San-ta Claus is com-in' to town. With

Music Box Chorus

lit-tle tin horns and lit-tle toy drums, Root-y-toot-toots and rum-my-tum-tums, San-ta Claus is com-in' to town. And cur-ly head dolls that

Santa Claus Is Comin' To Town

tod-dle and coo, El - e - phants, boats and kid-die cars too,

San - ta Claus is com - in' to town.

The Kids in Girl - and Boy - land will

have a jub - i - lee, They're gon - na build a

Toy - land town all a - round the Christ - mas tree, So! You

bet-ter watch out, you bet-ter not cry, Bet-ter not pout, I'm tell-ing you why:

San - ta Claus is com - in' to town.

2. Now San-ta is a bus-y man,
he has no time to play, He's
got mil-lions of stock-ings To
fill on Christ-mas day; You'd
bet-ter write your let-ter now
And mail it right a-way, Be-
cause he's get-ting read-y His
rein-deers and his sleigh, So,

Silent Night

Franz Gruber

1. Si - lent night,
2. *Stil - le Nacht,*

Ho - ly night! All is calm, all is bright,
hei - le - ge Nacht! Al - les schlaft, ein - sam wacht,

Silent Night

'Round yon Vir - gin Moth - er and Child. Ho - ly In - fant so
nur das trau - te hoch - hei - li - ge Paar. Hol - der Kna - be im

ten - der and mild, Sleep in heav - en - ly peace,
loc - ki-gen Haar, schlaf' in himm - li - scher Ruh',

Sleep in heav - en - ly peace!
schlaf' in himm - li - scher Ruh'!

Silent night, holy night!
Son of God, love's pure light,
Radiant beams from Thy holy face,
With the dawn of redeeming grace,
Jesus, Lord, at Thy birth,
Jesus, Lord, at Thy birth.

Silent night, holy night!
Shepherds quake at the sight,
Glories stream from heaven afar,
Heav'nly hosts sing Alleluia;
Christ, the Savior, is born,
Christ, the Savior, is born.

Sleigh Ride

Words by
MITCHELL PARISH

Music by
LEROY ANDERSON

CHORUS

Just hear those sleigh bells jin - gle - ing, ring - ting - tin - gle - ing,

too,_____ Come on, it's love - ly weath - er for a

SLEIGH RIDE to - geth - er with you,_____ Out - side the

Sleigh Ride

snow is fall-ing and friends are call-ing "Yoo hoo,"_____

Come on, it's love-ly weath-er for a SLEIGH RIDE to-geth-er with

you._____ Gid-dy - yap, gid-dy-yap, gid-dy -

yap, let's go, Let's look at the show,

We're rid-ing in a won-der-land of snow._____

Gid-dy-yap, gid-dy-yap, gid-dy - yap, it's grand,

Just hold-ing your hand, We're glid-ing a -

long with a song of a win-ter-y fair-y land, Our cheeks are

Sleigh Ride

nice and ros - y, and com - fy co - zy are we,____

We're snug - gled up to - geth-er like two birds of a feath-er would

be.____ Let's take that road be - fore us and

wing a chor-us or two,____ Come on, it's

To Interlude

1

love-ly weath-er for a SLEIGH RIDE to-geth-er with you.____ There's a

2 *Last time*   *Fine*

you.____

Interlude

birth - day par - ty at the home of Farm - er

Gray, It'-ll be the per - fect end - ing of a

per - fect day, We'll be sing - ing the songs we

77

Sleigh Ride

love to sing with-out a sin-gle stop, At the

fire - place while we watch the chest - nuts pop.

POP! POP! POP! There's a hap - py feel - ing noth - ing in the

world can buy, When they pass a - round the

cof - fee and the pump - kin pie, It' - ll

near - ly be like a pic - ture print by Cur - ri - er and

Ives, These won - der - ful things are the things we re -

mem - ber all thru our lives! Just hear those

D.S. al Fine

78

The Twelve Days of Christmas

English Carol

The Twelve Days of Christmas

par - tridge   in   a   pear   tree.   5. On the   fifth   day   of Christ - mas my

true love gave to   me   Five   gold - en   rings,

Four   call - ing birds,   Three French hens,   Two   tur - tle doves,   and a

par -   tridge   in   a   pear   tree.

6. On   the   sixth day of Christ-mas my true love gave to me   Six   geese a - lay - ing,

Five gold - en   rings,   Four   call - ing birds,   Three French hens,

Two   tur - tle doves, and a   par - tridge   in a pear   tree.   *D.S.*   tree.

The Twelve Days of Christmas

7. On the seventh day of Christmas my true love gave to me
   Seven swans aswimming,
8. On the eighth day of Christmas my true love gave to me
   Eight maids a milking,
9. On the ninth day of Christmas my true love gave to me
   Nine la-dies waiting,
10. On the tenth day of Christmas my true love gave to me
    Ten lords aleaping,
11. On the eleventh day of Christmas my true love gave to me
    'Leven pipers piping,
12. On the twelfth day of Christmas my true love gave to me
    Twelve drummers drumming,

Up On The Housetop

Written by B.R. Hanby

Introduction

1. Up on the house - top rein - deer pause,

Out jumps good old San - ta Claus; Down thro' the chim - ney with

lots of toys, All for the lit - tle ones' Christ - mas joys.

Ho, Ho, Ho! Who would-n't go! Ho, Ho, Ho!

Who would-n't go! Up on the house - top, click, click, click,

Up On The Housetop

Down   thro'   the   chim -   ney   with   good   Saint   Nick.

First comes the stocking of little Nell;
Oh, dear Santa, fill it well;
Give her a dollie that laughs and cries,
One that will open and shut her eyes.

Next comes the stocking of little Will;
Oh, just see what a glorious fill;
Here is a hammer and lots of tacks,
Also a ball and a whip that cracks.

We Three Kings

Words and music by John Hopkins

We Three Kings

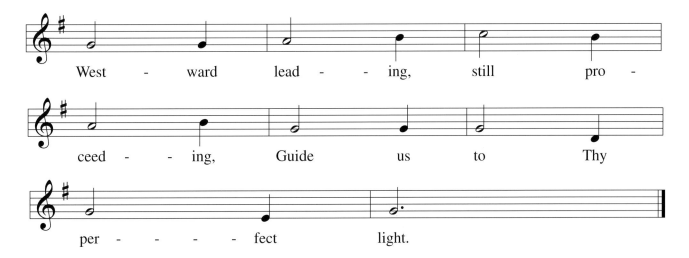

West - ward lead - - ing, still pro -
ceed - - ing, Guide us to Thy
per - - - - fect light.

Born a King on Bethlehem plain,
Gold I bring to crown Him again,
King forever, Ceasing never
Over us all to reign.
Chorus

Myrrh is mine; its bitter perfume
Breathes a life of gathering gloom;
Sorrowing, sighing Bleeding, dying,
Sealed in the stone cold tomb.
Chorus

Frankincanse to offer have I,
Incense owns a Deity night:
Prayer and praising, All men raising,
Worship Him, God on high.
Chorus

Glorious now behold Him arise,
King and God, and sacrifice;
Heaven sings Alleluia:
Alleluia the earth replies.
Chorus

We Wish You A Merry Christmas

Traditional English Carol

1.We wish you a Mer-ry Christ-mas, We wish you a Mer-ry

Christ-mas; We wish you a Mer-ry Christ-mas, And a

We Wish You A Merry Christmas

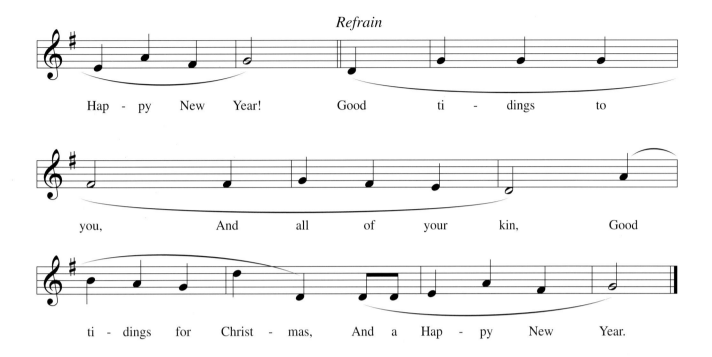

Oh, bring us some figgy pudding,
Oh, bring us some figgy pudding,
Oh, bring us some figgy pudding,
And bring it out here!
Refrain

We won't go until we got some,
We won't go until we got some,
We won't go until we got some,
So bring it right now!
Refrain

What Child Is This?

Traditional English Carol

What Child Is This?

Haste, haste to bring Him laud, The Babe, the Son of Mar - y!

Why lies He in such mean estate,
Where ox and ass are feeding?
Good Christian, fear: for sinners here,
The silent world is pleading:
Nails, spear, shall pierce Him through,
The Cross be born, for me, for you:
Hail, hail, the Word made flesh,
The Babe, the Son of Mary!

So bring Him incense, gold and myrrh,
Come peasant king to own Him,
The King of kings, salvation brings,
Let loving hearts enthrone Him.
Raise, raise the song on high,
The Virgin sings her lullaby:
Joy, joy, for Christ is born,
The Babe, the Son of Mary!

While Shepherds Watched Their Flocks

Nahum Tate

George F. Handel

1. While shep-herds watched their flocks by night, All seat-ed on the ground, The an-gel of the Lord came down, And glo-ry shone a-round, And glo-ry shone a-round.

"Fear not!" said He, for mighty dread
Had seized their troubled mind,
"Glad tidings of great joy I bring,
To you and all mankind,
To you and all mankind."

"To you, in David's town, this day
Is born of David's line
The Savior who is Christ the Lord,
And this shall be the sign,
And this shall be the sign."

"The Heav'nly Babe you there shall find
To human view displayed,
All meanly wrapped in swathing band
And in a manger laid,
And in a manger laid."

"All glory be to God on high,
And to the earth be peace,
Good will henceforth from heav'n to men,
Begin and never cease,
Begin and never cease."

Winter Wonderland

Words by
DICK SMITH

Music by
FELIX BERNARD

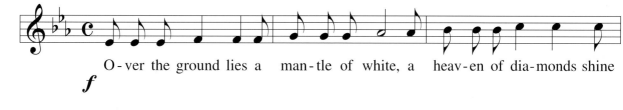

O-ver the ground lies a man-tle of white, a heav-en of dia-monds shine

f

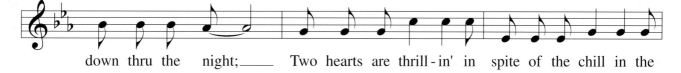

down thru the night;_____ Two hearts are thrill-in' in spite of the chill in the

Winter Wonderland

weath - er.   Love knows no sea - son;

love knows no clime;____ ro - mance can blos - som an - y old time;____

Here in the o - pen, we're walk - in' and hop - in' to - geth - er!____

1. Sleigh - bells ring, are you lis - t'nin'? In the

lane snow is glis - t'nin', a beau - ti - ful sight,____ we're

hap - py to - night, walk - in' in a win - ter won - der - land! Gone a-

way is the blue - bird, here to stay is a

new bird; He sings a love song,____ as we go a - long,____

walk - in' in a win - ter won - der - land!____ In the mead - ow we can build a

Winter Wonderland

snow-man, Then pre-tend that he is Par-son Brown;_____

He'll say, "Are you mar-ried?" We'll say, "No, man! But you can do the job when you're in

town!"_____ Lat-er on, we'll con - spire,_____ as we

dream by the fire,_____ to face un - a - fraid,_____ the

plans that we made, walk-in' in a win-ter won-der - land! Sleigh-bells land!_____

2. Sleigh-bells ring, are you lis-t'nin'?
   In the lane snow is glis-t'nin',
   a beau-ti-ful sight, we're hap-py to-night,
   walk-in' in a win-ter won-der-land!
   Gone a-way is the blue-bird
   here to stay is a new bird;
   He's sing-ing a song, as we go a-long,
   walk-in' in a win-ter won-der-land!
   In the mead-ow we can build a snow-man,
   And pre-tend that he's a cir-cus clown;
   We'll have lots of fun with Mis-ter Snow-man,
   Un-til the oth-er kid-dies knock 'im down!
   When it snows, ain't it thrill-in';
   Tho' your nose gets a chill-in'?
   We'll frol-ic and play the Es-ki-mo way,
   walk-in' in a win-ter won-der-land!

Photographic Credits